IMAGES
of Wales

UPPER RHONDDA
THE SECOND SELECTION

Mary Jane Berry lived at 6 Beynon Row and was the midwife for Blaencwm for many years; it is said that she was present at the birth of close on 5,000 babies. Mrs Berry was also the Mayoress of Blaencwm prior to the Second World War.

IMAGES
of Wales

UPPER RHONDDA
THE SECOND SELECTION

Compiled by
Emrys Jenkins and Roy Green

TEMPUS

Members of Treherbert youth centre painting the backdrop of the stage at Blaenrhondda Working Mens Club. The mural depicts some of the many photographs taken by the late Mr Jack Hart.

This book is dedicated to our children
Margaret, William, Ceri, Lynwen, Diane, Jeffrey and Phillip.

First published 1999
Reprinted 2004

Tempus Publishing Limited
The Mill, Brimscombe Port,
Stroud, Gloucestershire, GL5 2QG
www.tempus-publishing.com

© Emrys Jenkins and Roy Green, 1999

The right of Emrys Jenkins and Roy Green to be
identified as the Authors of this work has been
asserted in accordance with the Copyrights, Designs
and Patents Act 1988.

British Library Cataloguing in Publication Data.
A catalogue record for this book is available from the British Library.

ISBN 0 7524 1609 X

Typesetting and origination by Tempus Publishing Limited.
Printed in Great Britain.

Contents

Outside the grocers shop at No. 4 (or No. 5) Llewellyn Street, Blaencwm, *c.* 1917. In the photograph is Mr Tom Carpenter (owner) and left to right are: Elsie Carpenter, -?-, Doris Carpenter.

Emrys Jenkins, Will Scott, Roy Green.

Introduction

By William Scott

In writing this introduction to a new volume of old photographs I feel that the three most important factors that can make any book successful should be mentioned. Firstly, the subject: the Rhondda that is part of us, where we live, where most of us grew up, where we forged friendships, a place that we are asked about by people we meet on holidays and travel. 'Where are you from?', is the question, and the answer is said with pride, 'The Rhondda Valley'. When this subject is covered in book form it is read in all corners of the world by families who were born here and now live in distant parts. It will be enjoyed with the same mixture of emotion and nostalgia that we all feel. The second factor is the authors who seem to go on unearthing massive numbers of fresh photographs of our area and by displaying them like this with accompanying commentaries awaken memories for everyone. We can all enjoy sharing these memories with our families and friends as we recall activities and events we have in common with those whose photographs appear in this book.

For this we are grateful to Emrys Jenkins and Roy Green for their work in assembling this book, confident in the knowledge that their enjoyment in the task will be shared by those who read it. The third factor is the public: you and I, and all those who will enjoy the book. Age is no limitation for enjoyment, and if we the older generation are in the forefront at present, have no fear for the future decades because those coming behind us will also enjoy books of this kind, for books on the Rhondda are synonymous with all of our lives. Thank you for giving me the opportunity and the pleasure of writing this introduction.

The Authors

Emrys Jenkins was born in the Penyrenglyn area of Treherbert in 1930. He was educated in Penyrenglyn and Porth County schools where he was granted special dispensation to leave school at the early age of 14 $\frac{1}{2}$ years to start an apprenticeship as a toolmaker in the new HMV Gramophone Co. in Treorchy. On completion of his five year apprenticeship he joined the RAF in 1950 to serve his two years conscription. Following his demobilisation in 1952 he returned to his old company which had now changed its name to EMI. In 1962 he was promoted to Production Engineer and in 1970 to Quality Engineer. He retired in 1986 after workng forty one years with the company. As well as local history research his interests include gardening and photography. He regularly judges local horticultural shows and also the Rhondda-Cynon-Taff In Bloom competition.

Roy Green was born at No. 30 Eileen Place, Tynewydd in 1926 and has lived since 1956 at No. 42 Eileen Place. He started work in 1940 and worked in Tydraw, Glenrhondda, and Fernhill collieries before finishing in Fernhill in October 1973 due to ill-health. His working life was completed in the area offices of the Coal Board in Llanishen from where he retired in 1981. Since his retirement he has been interested in photography, gardening, and bowls, and was involved in the Down Memory Lane exhibitions held in the OAP Hall in Treherbert in the early 1990s. He shares with Emrys a strong interest in the history of the area and collecting old photographs of it.

Pentre Athletic AFC Second XI, 1949/50, holders of the Ely valley cup, Senior cup, UR Challenge cup, LR Championship cup, and the Lucania cup. Left to right, standing: W. French (trainer), D. Bartlett, Ron Jones, G. Payne, Reg Kearle, T. Ellis, Jack Childs, M. Rees. Seated: J. Murphy, P.K. Jones, Bryn Edwards (captain), I. Morgan, Tommy Morgan.

One
Blaenrhondda

General view of Blaenrhondda, *c.* 1920.

Outside the Blaenrondda Hotel (The Kick), 1925. Left to right: Nellie Davies, Glanville Walters, Dilwyn Davies (landlord), Arthur Davies, John Richards ('Shoni Fish', local fishmonger).

An early photograph of Blaenrhondda, c. 1885. Caroline Street and Blaenrhondda can be seen in the background. Note that Brook Street below the school has not yet been built.

Class 1 Blaenrhondda infants' school, 1913.

Caroline football team, c. 1920. Left to right, back row: Moses Davies, Dan Jones, Ray Mears, -?-, Tom Lewis, Jonah Lewis, Will Sampson, Will Lewis, Tom Shanklyn, Tom Beard. Front row: Joe Jones, Fred Woolfe, Tom Lewis, Jim Llewellyn, Dick Evans.

Mr Mort's chauffeur Jimmy Jones with a Calthorpe car outside Fernhill house. Mr Mort was the agent/manager of Fernhill colliery.

General view of Blaenrhondda looking towards the colliery. Note the line of coal trucks and Fernhill houses in the background.

Officials of Messers W.M. Treglown and council officials opening valve house and pipeline at the south entrance of the Blaenrhondda to Llyn reservoir tunnel in 1910. On the left hand side can be seen the 22inch pipeline supported and armoured against frost by reinforced concrete, the aquaduct pillar is built on a bed of rock.

The entrance to Scwd level at the top end of Blaenrhondda, c. 1900. The old boiler can still be seen on site.

Blaenrhondda Hotel darts team, *c.* 1933. Left to right, back row: Wilf Fussel, Harry Phipps, Harry Bishop, Charlie Phipps, Ned Davies, Will Lewis. Middle row: Tommy Davies (Day), Wylie Pearce, Tom Tal Williams, Dick Jones, Dan Morgan. Front row: Morgan Thomas, Joe Davies (Bach), Aron Jones, Billo Owen.

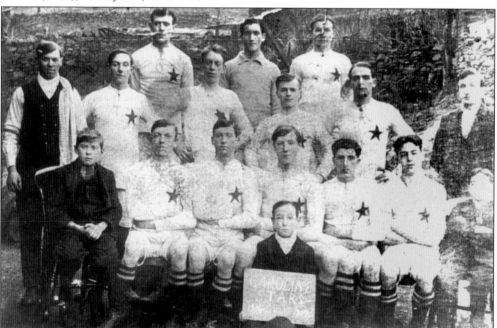

Caroline Stars football team, 1916/17. Left to right, back row: Ray Mears, Tom Beard, Albert Mitchel. Middle row: Jim Lewis, Will Hawkins, Len Goodman, Jonah Davies, -?-, Fred Hawkins. Front row: Tom Lewis, W.H. Williams, Alf Hawkins, -?-, -?-, Llew Phillips, -?-. The boy in front is Harry Hawkins.

Caroline Street was demolished in 1976.

Floods in Brook Street in 1960.

Residents of Caroline Street, left to right, back row: George Mears, Tommy Watkins, Iory Sampson, Albert Gardner. Front row: Dabo Powell, Fred Gardner, Tom Gardner.

Clarion Cycling Club. Left to right, back row, Tom Gardner, Clarence Jacka, Dai Jacka, Elwyn Davies, Tom Carpenter. Middle row: Rollo Davies, Tom Bibey, Haydn Jones, Glyn John, Vernon Rees. Front row: Will Sampson, Harry Sampson, -?-.

Blaenrhondda rugby team at the opening of the Blaenrhondda field by T.L. Mort, agent/manager for Fernhill Collieries, 28 October 1920. Included in the photograph are: Dennis Donovan, W. Harris, Moses Rees, E. Thomas, W. Lewis, Tom Bowen, Con Griffiths, Albert Mitchel, D. Morley, Morgan Jones, Tommy Cox, B. Haddrel, Tom Spiller, S. Holder, E. Smith. Blaenrhondda beat Treorchy All Whites 6-0.

Fernhill colliery stores. In the middle are, left to right: Des Morgan (storekeeper), Barry Owen (assistant), Joe Jones. The two other men are area auditors.

Fernhill colliery 1956. Note Blaenrhondda farm in the top right hand corner.

Fernhill Colliery fire fighting team, 1966. Left to right, back row: Dai Edwards, Gwyn Gardner, Gwyn Phillips (captain), Brian Morgan, Bob Berry, Terry Collinson. Front row: Will Purdell, Roy Green, D.J. Hughes (manager), Fred Woods, Gus Broughton. The team were winners of the underground team and the two-man Area 3 team competition and also winners of the South Western Division final.

Fernhill Presentation Supper at the 'Top Club'. Left to right, back row: Don Bundock, Roy Green, Dai Davies (Wyers), D.J. Hughes (manager), Danny Morris, George Rees, Cliff True. Front row: -?-, Harry Morgan, Jim Squires, -?-, Will Lazarus, -?-, Stan Provis.

Fernhill ladies choir in 1950.

Fernhill Houses residents VE day celebrations in 1945.

Blaenrhondda AFC, 1951/52. Left to right, back row: Trevor Lewis, W.G.(Dixie) Lewis, -?-, Danny Jones, David Carpenter, Peter Morgan, Ralph Phillips, Harry Williams, Paul Thomas, Jim Squires (referee). Front row: Dickie Jones, John Lee, Jim Sampson, Ray Luckwell, Ken Phillips, Dennis Phillips, Edgar Evans, Tomos Sampson, W.G. 'Fudgy' Lewis. The boys in front are Terry Lewis and Ceri Lewis.

Fernhill Colliery, No. 1 shaft (left) and No. 2 shaft (right). Caroline Street is visible in the background.

Fernhill Colliery, No 1 and 2 shafts. The headgear of No 1 shaft collapsed one Sunday morning in 1968 while the shaft was being filled.

The presentation to Derek Jenkins on his retirement as a mechanic at Fernhill Colliery. Left to right, back row: Emlyn Evans, Haydn Morgan, Cyril Pratt, Roy Green, Griff Leek, Arthur Thomas (manager), Charles Jenkins. Front row: Jack Lewis, Derek Jenkins, Jack Widdiecombe.

Fernhill Colliery maintenance staff. Left to right, back row: Will Evans, Ted Irons, David Pritchard, -?-, -?-, Graham Howells, Ron Demaid, Mansel Cox, Freddy Hayward. Second row: Ivor Aubrey, Howard Davies, Cyril Pratt, Rhys Williams, Fred Woods. Third row: Dai Carpenter, Idwal Llewellyn, Jack Pratt, Benny Pratt, Tommy Morse, T.G. Williams. Front row: Gerald Bees, Dai Rees, Des Rees, Dilwyn Jones, Norman Davies.

The Carnival Queen, 1948/49. Left to right: Joan Bowen, Doreen Beasley (queen), Ray Jones, Rene Richards, Maureen Locke.

A view of Blaenrhondda with Tydraw colliery in the foreground and on the left are Graig-y-Ddelw houses which had just been completed.

Two colliers and a collier boy coming off their shift at Fernhill colliery, *c.* 1920. The collier on the right is Edwin Beard.

The demolition of a chimney stack at Fernhill colliery, 1965.

Two

Blaencwm

'The Square', with Deulwen Terrace in the background.

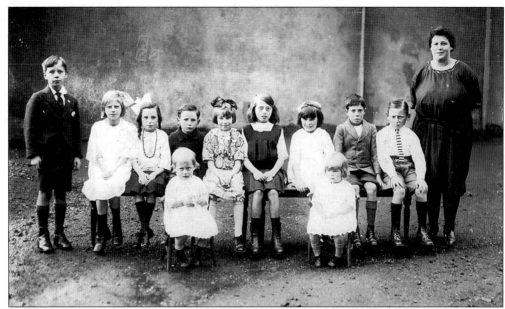

Blaencwm Sunday school class, 1922/3. Left to right: Tommy Carpenter, Ruby Jones, Vi Nash, Cyril Nash, -?-, -?-, -?-, -?-, Jack Morgan, Gwyneth Jones (née Widow), teacher. The two girls in the front are not known.

Blaencwm school, 1928/29. Included in the photograph are: Cyril Nash, Oliver Ruddock, Irene Evans, Lucy Parry, Evelyn Parry.

St David's concert. Included in the photo are: Jake Phillips, Lennie Griffiths, Ron Berry, Elton Merry, Bryn Lisle, Cissy Parsons, Fred Evans, Lily Phillips, Freda Vickery, ? Smallridge, Muriel Mitchell, Eirwen Brunker, ? Holland and two sisters named Pickens.

Tydraw Colliery in 1919.

A skiffle group from Blaencwm Maes-yr-Haf who met in Glenrhondda Institute 1957. Left to right, standing: Teg Duggan, Bessie Lewis, Ada Morgan, Bessie Edwards, Vi Davies, Mair Rees, Ena Parry, Marion Nash, Vi Brunker, Phyllis Turner. Kneeling: Glenys Richards, Elsie Adams, Ethel Benning, Mrs Wessendorf (standing behind drum).

A view of Dunraven school with Tydraw Colliery on the left and Blaencwm in the background. Trem-y Glyn house can be seen on the right hand side.

Blaencwm girls club in 1945. Left to right, back row: Mattie Morgan -?-, Mair Jones. Middle row: Gladys Ellis, Daisy Pritchard, -?-, Rivella Shinborne, Shirley Wessendorf, -?-. Front row: -?-, Loice Jones, Kitty Williams, Mrs Berry (leader), Irene Pickens, Mary Jones, Glenys Vaughan. The club was started in the early years of the Second World War by Mrs Berry and they met in the upstairs room of the Hendrewen Hotel.

Selsig Amateur Operatic Society performing *The Mikado* at the Palace cinema in 1960.

Dai Evans and Ron Galloway in the powerhouse of Glenrhondda Colliery in 1961.

Frank Locke, winding engineman in the winding engine house of the new pit at Glenrhondda colliery, in 1961.

Blaencwm School in 1962. Left to right, back row: Ralph Bobbett, Michael Morgan, Kevin Thomas, Brian Phillips, David Pate, Stewart Hughes, -?-, Mark Jones, David Nash. Middle row: Malcolm White, -?-, John Pate, Dawn Richards, Helen Brunker, Susan Switton. Front row: Leigh Richards, Julie Hunt, Lynnette Sealey, Lynne Edwards, Helen Pickens, Julie Nash, Sharon Dobb, Sandra Bundock, Janet Pearce, Carolyn Switton.

Glenrhondda Colliery retirement party in 1964. Left to right, back row: Mel Rawlins, Gordon Rogers, Fred Richardson, Cliff Hobbs (Lodge chairman), Hiley Jones, Wally Evans, Jack Thomas (Ty-Glas), Walt Parfitt. Front row: Ossie Biggs, -?-, Tom Richards, Dai Williams, Will Peachey.

Blaencwm School Play in 1958. From left to right, Peter Richardson, -?-, Barry Jones, John Vaughan, June Parry, followed by the three Jones boys, John Richardson.

Blaencwm AFC Lower Rhondda cup winners, 1960/61. Left to right, back row: Terry Collinson, Wynford Rossiter, Des Owen, Clive Jones, Gerwyn Griffiths, Ian Searle. Front row: Brian Rees, Gwyn Phillips, Haydn Lewis, Brian Pritchard, John Jones.

Blaencwm Killties Jazzband in 1952. Left to right, back row: Margaret Pritchard, Ray Jones, Ruby Sealey, Pat Swift, Pat Jones. Middle row: Wendy Eastman, Joyce Spurway, Mair Pritchard, Margaret Potter, Pat Carpenter, Pat Hicks, Pat Phillips. Front row: Pat Duggan, Christine Peasley, Myra Pritchard, Eirwen Phillips (leader), Ann Mundy, Mary Baker, Sandra Hughes. On drums: Maralyn Richards, Shirley Gregory, Yvonne Rees. (Perhaps it should have been called 'Pats' band!)

Children of Junior Mixed School, St Davids Day, 1966. Left to right, back row: Martin Harry, Mark Barnes, Clive Smith, Jeffrey Mackee, Malcolm White, Michael Pearce, Ian Culverhouse, Stephen Price, Stephen Parry. Front row: Helen Phillips, Kay Pritchard, Sharon Dobbs, Diane Thomas, Lorraine Davies, Christine Evans, Kim James, Janine George.

Tommy Carpenter, leader of the local accordian band.

Three
Tynewydd

Wyndham Street, c. 1900. Note the absence of the Tydraw Institute (now Treherbert rugby club) on the left hand side.

Mrs Mary Smith of 46 Margaret Street, Tynewydd, was born in Tredegar but left there at an early age to live in the Rhondda. At eleven years of age she began work in a brickyard and toiled for eleven hours a day for the sum of two shillings and ten pence. At fifteen years of age Mrs Smith was turning out 1,500 bricks per day herself and was paid five shillings per week. (It is said that these bricks were made at the side of the stream at the top of Alma Street, if this is correct it may be the reason why the Tynewydd Hotel is called 'The Bricks'). She also worked on the surface of the Tynewydd colliery at the time when many women were employed to work on colliery surfaces. Interviewed by a *Rhondda Leader* reporter she gave an interesting light on how the beer trade was conducted in the Rhondda in the early part of this century. The trade was not then licensed and pints of beer were given free if one bought three Spanish nuts (peanuts) for three old pence at the public house.

School Queen, 1933/34. The queen is Pauline Jones and included in the picture are Ellen Richards, Mrs Hinds-Arnold, Eunice Davies, Ruth Jones, Daphne Green.

A performance of the *Birth of Christ* by members of Ebeneezer chapel, 1927. Left to right, back row: -?-, Rhiannon Griffiths, Nora Kinsey. Middle row: Minnie Ryan, Nancy Roderick, Eirwen Harris, Marie Saunders, Gwenny Harris, Eunice Jones, May Saunders, Annie May Jones. Front row: Megan Jones, Dilys Davies, Glenys Farnham, Miss Abrahams, Carlotta Saunders, Doris Hammond.

Stephen and Margaret Jane Parry of 61 Eileen Place, *c.* 1927. Stephen migrated from near Aberystwyth to work in the mines, and Margaret came from Trelewis.

The upper end of Wyndham Street, *c.* 1920. Note the Ebeneezer chapel in the background, rebuilt in 1928. John Davies the newsagent is on the right hand side. Note the tramway loop to facilitate the passing of trams.

Wyndham Street, *c.* 1912.

General view of Tynewydd. Note Tynewydd cottage on the left, Tynewydd farm in the centre, and what is thought to be the Tynewydd colliery office on the right of the farm.

Garden Village, built to house Fernhill colliery officials and now known as Castleton Avenue. Fernhill house, the home of agent/manager Trevor L. Mort ME, JP can be seen in the background.

The Palace cinema was destroyed by fire at 5pm on Monday 25 March 1985.

Minister and deacons of Ebeneezer chapel 1932. From left to right, back row: M.I. Williams, O. Jones, W. Morgan, S. Williams, H. Mainwaring, A. Jones. Front row: T. Roderick, E. Davies, M. Owen (minister), D. Jones, D. Price.

Ebeneezer Sunday school, *c.* 1923. From left to right, back row: Annie May Jones, Eirwen Harris. Front row: Mair Edmunds, Tegwen Evans, Annie Hughes, Beryl Cassam, Megan Jones.

Children of Eileen Place, *c.* 1925. In the photograph are Lottie Williams, Eva Snell, Glyn Williams, George Edwards, Lilian Davies(holding baby), Violet Davies, Haydn Harris, Myra Evans, Rene Powell, Esme Jones, Jack Snell, Trevor Snell, Ossie Snell, Gomer Davies, Lilly Oliver, Haydn Williams, Dilwyn Williams, Dorothy Davies, Doris Hammond, Gwyneth Evans and Eirwen Davies.

Members of Hope chapel 1947/48. The ladies, from left to right: Mrs Davies, Mrs Price, Mrs Parsons, Mrs Webb, Mrs Provis, Mrs Williams. The men, left to right; -?-, Stan Provis, Mr Baker-Jones. The two men at the front are not known.

Members of Hope chapel at the re-opening after repairs 1947/48. Left to right, back row: Jinnie Evans, Barbara Evans, Phyllis Evans, Mrs Provis, -?-, Mrs Williams, Mabel Parsons. Second row: Mrs Price, Mrs Bell, Mrs Davies, Mrs Webb, Bessie Webb, Phyllis Perkins, Freda Watts, Mrs Morgan, Pheobe Roberts, Mr Baker-Jones. Third row: Mrs Stonier, Mrs Davies, Mrs Williams, Mrs Perkins, Mrs Davies, Mrs Haddock, Amy Perkins, Mr Morgan. Front row: Mr Galloway, Mrs Parsons, Mrs Davies, Mrs Davies, Terry Davies, -?-, Esme Provis, -?-, Frank Haddock.

Mrs Davies of 18 Halifax Terrace, 5 February 1913.

Revd and Mrs Cynon Evans of Blaencwm chapel, photographed on their Golden Wedding day in August 1936.

Brands Hatch in Eileen Place 1954. From front to back, Diane Green, Alan O'Leary, Howard O'Leary, Bryn Thomas.

Gelli Toreadors jazzband marching past
the Wyndham Hotel during the 1926
miners' strike. Note the Emporium shop
and the tramcar in the background.

Blaenrhondda station. Note the wooden platform on the right hand side.

Tydraw colliery officials presentation to Morgan Jones on his retirement 1953. From left to right, Harry Cull, Harry Cull (Jnr), Mike Meek, Morgan Jones, Islwyn Phillips, Eddy Pugh (manager), Roy Green, Ivor Roles, John Richards, Cyril Smart, -?-, Reg Powell, Jack Rees.

A mineral train from Fernhill colliery. Notice the houses of Upper St Albans Road in the background – now demolished.

Dunraven infants school, Class 3, 1931. From left to right, back row: Miss Griffiths, Raymond White, Benny Pratt, Ken Jones, Emrys Harris, -?-, Ivor Vaughan, Idris Moxy, Vincent Thomas, Henry King, Cyril Husband, Jack Smart, Dai Fitzpatrick, Rufus Harris. Middle row: -?-, -?-, Vera Vaughan, -?-, -?-, -?-, -?-, Rita Peasley, -?-, Mona Williams, Nancy Fry, Margaret Jones, Valmau Jones, Nita Griffiths. Front row: -?-, Cliff Doughty, Olga Woolfe, -?-, Jean Richards, Peggy Davies, Lil Jones, Plennydd Jackson, Gwyn Jones, Willie R. Davies, Dillwyn Green.

St Albans church juvenile choir, 1928.

Dunraven school 1935. Included in the photograph are, Eddy Phillips, Jessie Doughty, Frank Read, Muriel Guy, Charlie Goodman, John Griffiths, Gordon Evans, Marion Jones, Billy Farmer.

Dunraven school 1927. From left to right, back row: Winnie Williams (teacher), Tegwen Rees, Ivy Davies, Molly Eynon, Morfydd Evans, Nan Bryant, Lily Lang, Anni May Jones. Second row: Gracie Richards, Megan Edwards, Lal Williams, Emma Brymmer, Edith Evans, Maisie Purdell. Third row: Mavis Brown, Olwen Jones, Doris Harris. Fourth row, Ann Jenkins, Sybil White, Edna Richards, Audrey Miles, Nora Pratt, Doris Col. On right hand side, from front to back; Beryl Edwards, Maggie Riley, Mabel Jones, Edna Hughes, Mary Sampson.

Durnraven infants school 1936. From left to right, back row: Brian Fews, Towyn Davies, Idris Squires, Ionawr Richards, Wynford Harris, Gwyn Jones, Myrddin Jenkins, Gwyn Jones, Pat Burke, Norman Coles, Ken Sealey, Brian Hoffman. Middle row: -?-, Russel Smart, -?-, Gwilym Parfitt, Maldwyn Sampson, Dave Jones, Gary Williams, Gwyn Evans, Trevor Roderick, -?-, Graham Bowen, Roy Jones, John Hunt, -?-, Brian Peasley, Lilian Rees. Front row: Marion Warren, Metty Myring, Glenys Ellis, Annie Cude, Olwen Rees, Nancy Wellsford, Miriam Jackson, -?-.

Dunraven Mixed School, Standard 1V 1936. From left to right, back row: Mr Jones(teacher, known as 'Bulldog'), Vincent Thomas, Ken King, -?-, Gladys Thomas, -?-, Olga Woolfe, Iris Evans, Gwenno Coles, -?-, -?-, Stan Cox, -?-. Second row: Gerald Harris, Vi Svendsen, Rita Peasley, Marion Kinsey, -?-, Gladys Bignell, Marion Williams, -?-, Vera Vaughan, -?-, Howell Andrews, Hector Bevan. Front row: Billy Doughty, Des Williams, Roy Green, William G. Davies, Haydn Parfitt, Graham Cook, William M. Davies, George Sykes, Dyson Evans, William R. Davies.

Dunraven school 1936. From left to right, back row: Charlie Goodman, Elwyn Richards, -?-, Howard Biggs, Jeffrey Gilbert, Ivor Vaughan, -?-, Jimmy Squires. Second row: Billy Farmer, Ivy Hunt, -?-, Peggy Spurrey, -?-, Thelma James, -?-, -?-, -?-. Third row: Megan Harris, Marjorie Kinsey, Mary Williams, Rona Rees, Jessie Doughty, -?-, Marion Jones, Muriel Guy, Ruby Chitty, -?-, Miss Jones (teacher). Front row: Roy Davies, Cliff Morgan, Fred Thomas, Gordon Evans, Idwal Wallace, -?-, -?-.

Dunraven school, Standard 3A, 1936. From left to right, back row: Bobby Baker, Syd Parry, Eric Hoffman, Russ Howells, Ivor Griffiths, Ivor Thomas, Trevor Brymmer, Danny Donovan. Second row: Cecil Edwards (teacher), Ellen Richards, Peggy Howells, Nancy Mason, June Carrol, Velma Evans, Megan Edmunds, Mary Hannah Williams, Gwen Edmunds, Eirwen Williams, Beryl Colville. Third row: Bayne Denby, Joan Rees, Cissie Sampson, Doreen Smart, Kitty Thomas, Stella Davies, Betty Thompson, Winnie Davies, Linda Bailey. Front row: David Thomas, Teddy Morris, Colin Griffiths, Ken Jones, Frank Read, Cecil Pritchard.

Len Jones earned his place in Rhondda's boxing hall of fame. During his impressive boxing career he fought Jackie Turpin in Judge's Hall in the 1940s, he also fought Danny O'Sullivan, British Bantam Weight champion, Vernon Ball, and Ivor Davies of Neath in an eliminator for the championship of Wales. He also fought Tommy Macgovern, champion of Ireland, and his last fight was against Glyn Davey of Maesteg, champion of Wales.

Workmen of Tynewydd Colliery. The third man from the left is William Joseph. This colliery was opened in 1865 and was situated on top of the tips behind Treherbert rugby field.

St Albans church choir, 1929. Choirmaster was W. Herbert Jones and organist H.M. Austin. Included in the photograph are George Wooton Snr and George Wooton Jnr, Danny Wootton and Tom Broome.

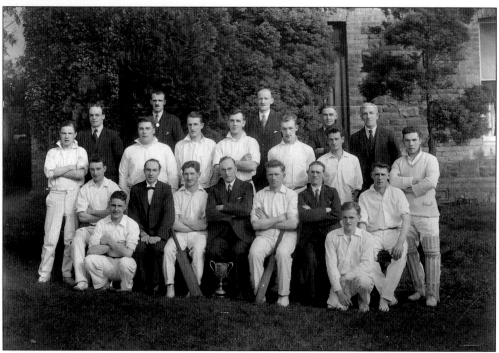

Tynewydd Cricket Club 1930. From left to right, back row: D. Rees. G. Goodridge, B. Griffiths, R. Hammond, D. Martin. Second row: E.J. Jones, E. Jones, C. Harris. B. Thomas, H. Harris, C. Rees, D. Martin. Front row: T. Davies, J.M. Phelps (chairman), A. Gruar (captain), T.L. Davies ME (president), G. Bush (vice captain), H. Harries (treasurer), E. Thomas (secretary).`Kneeling: A. Lewis, W. Hambury.

Tynewydd AFC (known as Stonetown). Lower Rhondda League Champions 1946/47. From left to right, back row: Des Williams, Eddy Warren, Danny Jones, Walt Chick, Ronnie Smart, Peter Morgan, Haydn (Dicky) Evans, Ivor Rossiter, Will Jenkins, Don Bundock, Emrys Warren. Front row: Howard Phillips, Bobby Morgan, Dick Jones, Islwyn Sampson, John Morgan, Mal Sampson, Thomas Sampson.

A view of Tynewydd taken from Pen-Pych mountain. Note the long curve of the Rhondda – Swansea Bay railway on the left and, just to the left of centre, the straight mineral railway that fed Fernhill and Tydraw collieries. Where this line forks it is possible to see a line of trucks going to Tydraw and also the large pond that was between the two lines. This has now been levelled to enable the extension to the factory to be built. Tydraw colliery rubbish bunker is visible on the right hand side of the picture.

A view of Tynewydd showing Dunraven school in the left hand corner, Tydraw colliery is in the background, Trem-y-glyn house by the side of the railway, Glenrhondda institute just to the right and in front of the village of Blaencwm.

Looking North to Blaenrhondda railway station. Notice the Palace cinema at the furthest end of the station and Blaenrhondda signal box on the right hand side.

Four
Treherbert

Treherbert railway station, 1883.

Treherbert boys' school, c. 1905.

Treherbert boys' school, 1908.

Benjamin John and his son Richard Henry John, 84 Dumfries street, coming off their shift at Abergorky colliery, *c.* 1914.

George Galloway and family. George was born in Kinross Scotland, and was brought by his parents to the Rhondda when he was three years of age. They lived in a cottage on Cwmsaerbren farm, the father was a bailiff, he was also named George, and was one of the founder members of Wesleyan chapel. Mrs Galloway came from Axebridge in Somerset. In the photograph are daughter Agnes, and sons George, John and William Henry.

The committee of Treherbert rugby team, when the team played on Cwmsaerbren field, the site of the present Treherbert park. From left to right, back row: Tom Anfield, -?-, -?-, -?-, Emlyn Lewis, Wally Thomas (Crown Hotel), Middle row: Dick Harris, John Todd-Jones, George Kirkhouse, Alfie Hitchings, -?-, -?-, Will Morgan (Corner House Hotel). Front row: Johnny Vaughan, -?-, Collins (Castle Hotel), ? Glass (ironmonger), Sydney Mainwaring, ? Biggs, Evan Hopkins.

Royal visit 27 June 1912. King George V and Queen Mary talking to RUDC chairman Thomas Evans JP on the platform of Treherbert station.

The Jordan Family who lived at No.1 Station Terrace, *c.* 1898. From left to right: Millicent, Jessie, Edith, Martha (mother), Charles, Clara, Alfred Ernest (father), Mabel, Theresa. Alfred was the Traffic Manager of Taff Vale railway.

Treherbert Thursdays RFC, 1919/20. From left to right, back row: E. Price, D.J. Williams, H. Galloway, Cliff Duckworth, Jason Thomas, David Woods, Len Trew, David Edwards. Second row: Will Evans, Jack Davies, T. Miles, Ivor Evans, D.V. Jones, Tom Griffiths, D. James, David Millward, Tom Thomas, Evan Morgan. Third row: Ivor Benbow, Eli Thomas, M.J. Ryan, H. Eveleigh (captain), Will Saunders, Ron Rees, G. Miles. Front row: Mor. Jones, Tom Owen, Mansell Cullen.

Standard 1 at Treherbert boys' school, 1913.

Libanus chapel, *c.* 1920. In the gateway are John Lewis and his grandsons John Lewis (left) and William John Jenkins (right).

The Rhondda Valleys Breweries Company with workmen and delivery lorry in the Treherbert yard to the rear of Station Street.

General view of Treherbert, *c.* 1900. Lady Margaret colliery is in the foreground.

Bute Street, *c.* 1938. On the left are shops owned by Richards (chemist) and Hancocks and on the right hand side are the Gaiety cinema, the Castle Hotel and the Corn Stores.

The Gaiety cinema, August 1938.

Bute Street, *c*. 1950.

Treherbert AFC, in the Welsh National League, 1921/22.

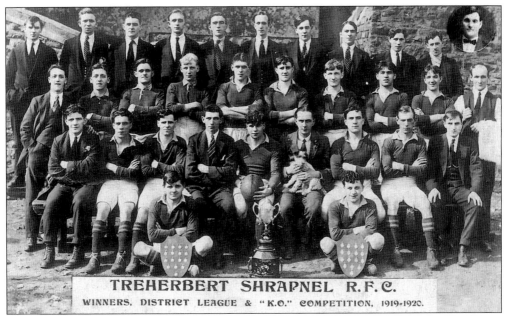

Treherbert Shrapnel RFC, winners of the District League and 'K.O.' Competition, 1919/20.

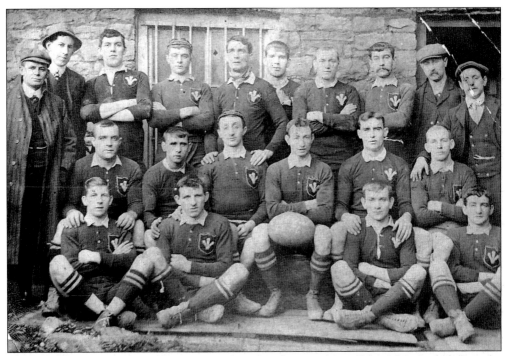

Treherbert Rugby League side 1907/08 who played Australia and lost 6-3. Included in the photograph is Rhys Morgan Rees, Dai Galloway, Harry Cox, George Eveleigh, Danny Fitzgerald (captain).

Treherbert Cooperative Guild, 1928.

May Williams (née Morgan) and May Owen (née Reynolds), members of the Treherbert Operatic society, performing in HMS *Pinafore* at the opera house, February 1912.

Treherbert Girls Friendly Society held under the auspices of St Mary's church, 1935/36. From left to right, middle row: Rosie Crane, Ethel Pickens, Lilwen Jones, Gladys Pickens, Miss Morgan, Annie May Jones. Kneeling: Marie Saunders, -?-, -?-.

Treherbert Girls Friendly Society sewing class. From left hand corner, clockwise: Lilwen Jones, Marie Saunders, Annie May Jones, Ethel Pickens, Gladys Pickens, Annie Hunt, Rosie Crane, Mair Herbert, -?-, Margaret Jayne, (Leader), -?-, Gwethyn Herbert, -?-.

Treherbert Hospital Committee, 1932. Included in the photograph are, Miss C. Morris (matron), E.J. Williams DC, Rhys Morgan Rees DC, Mrs G.C. Beavis, Mrs D. Cook, D. Jones, W.J. Pearce, W.J. Gruar, R.Williams, E. Jones, Gwilym Lloyd, T. Thomas, E. Henry, T. Anfield.

Staff of Treherbert Hospital, 1932. From left to right: Nurses Mary Olwen Williams, Margaret Griffiths, Sister Eva Ann Lewis, Nurse Ceinwen Griffiths, Matron Morris, Sister Gwenllian Burton, Nurses Evans and Hilda Polsom.

Treherbert Hospital, 1930.

Treherbert Hospital Committee, 1948. From left to right, back row: D.W. Griffiths, T. Duggan, D. Davies, T. Perkins, J. Davies, E. Jones, J. Andrews, W. Parfitt, E. Jones. Second row: R. Hammond, E. Gibby, Mrs J.M. Lewis, Miss Cove-Williams, Mrs R.Colwill, Mrs G.W. Luck, Miss T. Rees, Miss G. Thomas, G.W. Luck, T. Roderick, S. Jones. Front row: J.M. Williams, E. Henry, T. Anfield, L. Lewis, Mrs E.A. Wills (matron), E.J. Williams DC, R. Williams, W. Llewellyn CC, T. Roderick. The dog was called Danny.

Rabbiotti Bros refreshment rooms, 171 Bute street, *c.* 1920. The men were probably waiting for the charabanc before going on an outing to the races.

Bethany Baptist chapel Sunday school class. From left to right, back row: Tom Morgan, -?-, Jack Addis, -?-, -?-, -?-, -?-, Mr Davies, -?-, Gilbert Soley, David John Cole. Front row: George Edwards, Picton Cole, Tom Anfield, Mr Gray, Stanley Edwards, -?-, Mr Goodridge.

Emmanuel chapel nativity play, Christmas 1935. From left to right, standing: Beatrice Pickens, Sue Noble, Mr Rees (minister). Seated and kneeling: Eric Waters, John Fairchild, Ken Oram, Malcolm Gronow, Violet Dutfield, Freda Travess, Beryl Needhall, Des Jones, Reg Thomas, Cyril John.

St Johns Ambulance Corps, c. 1945. In the second row from the back are Nellie Davies, Betty Griffiths, Glyn Williams, Dai Thomas. In the third row from the back (right of centre) is Harry Hughes (cashier, Glenrhondda colliery) with Mrs Hughes on his right and Tom Richards on his left. On the front row the young man out of uniform is Ron Hammond.

Wesleyan chapel Fireside Fellowship, 1948/49. From left to right, back row: -?-, Mary Roberts, Olwen Davies, Gay Haddrell, -?-, Margaret Jones, Gwyneth Noble, Louie Chislett, Iris Morgan, -?-, Glenys Harris. Middle row: -?-, Vera Myring, Gwynvyl Evans, Rita Peasley, -?-, Muriel Snell, Betty Todd-Jones, Mary Greenhill, Edna Guy, Olwen Hopkins, -?-, Nancy Bryant, -?-. Front row: Nellie Richards, Betty Evans, Kitty Scott, Ira Yeoman, Mrs Avery, Olive Jones, Nellie Wallace, Peggy Bailey, Megan Hughes, Beryl Wootton.

A performance of *Ali Baba* by members of the Wesleyan chapel, *c*. 1935. From left to right, back row: Dick Bara Gwenydd, Glyn Hart, Les Vaughan, Will Colwille, Will Phelps, -?-, John Phelps, -?-, Viv Hoskings. Third row: Bert Price, Tommy Harris, Jessie Parsons, Cecil Harris, Frank Bayliss, Walt Phelps, Evan Jones, Tom Jones. Second row: Roy Harris, Ken Morgan, Dick Kinsey, Eddy Hoskings, Jim Phelps, Arthur Phelps, Mr Pritchard, -?-, Noah Griffiths. Front row: Kathleen Harris, Jack Arundel, Wesley Warman, Viv Evans, Mrs Pritchard, Will Morgan.

A public meeting held on the Treherbert-Rhigos road to discuss the permanent closure of the road due to subsidance. The road was closed on 12 February 1992.

Cyril Lewis (left) and Roy Green in the 'Hole' – created in the road by the subsidence. After extensive works the road was re-opened in May 1992.

Bethany Baptist chapel Womens League, *c.* 1950. From left to right, back row: May Edwards, Chloe Parry, Ruth Williams, Lily May Morgan, Martha Haddrell, Ethel Anfield, K.M. Thomas, Mrs Murray, -?-. Third row: Mrs Elliott, Mrs Cullen, Mrs Henry, Ethel Davies, Annie Davies, Minnie Griffiths. Second row: -?-, Ginny Gibson, Mrs Goodridge, -?-. Front row: Katie Barret, Rhoda Morgan, Mrs Parry.

Treherbert Senior Girls School, 1936. From left to right, back row: Miss Bessie Evans, Ada Doughty, Melba Warman, Eileen Evans, Burl Morgan, Beryl Chivers, Gwen Sheppard, Sylvia Richards, -?-, -?-, Rosie Escott. Middle row: Miss Tynan, Cridwen Williams, Doreen Moore, -?-, Marjorie Lodwig, Glenys Barret, Joan Watts, Beryl Gruar, Elvira Henry, -?-, Front row: -?-, Miss Samuels, -?-, -?-, Margaret Watkins, Vera Davies, Violet Thomas, -?-, Joan Jackson, -?-.

The carnival queen and her entourage, 1936. From left to right: Hilda Berry, Blod Perkins, Margaret James, Morfydd Davies (queen), Rena Jones, Cridwen Jones, Joyce Howells. The two little girls in front are Rose Hunt and Margaret Haddrell. The two boys are unknown.

Bethany Baptist chapel Nativity Play, 1947. From left to right, back row: Graham John, Berwyn Hughes, Revd W.H. Davies, Emlyn Thomas, Edgar Jones, Jack Hughes, Wyn Cullen, John Walters (black face). Third row: Ann Benbow, Audrey James, Burl Morgan, Myra Thomas, Dorothy Hughes. Second row: Nesta James, Doreen James, Dilys James, Hilary Lancey, Rita Bowen. Front row: Maureen Thomas, Pat Morris, Pat Thomas.

A bowls presentation at Treherbert park. From left to right: Will John Davies, Tudor James, George Edwards, Ben Evans, -?-, -?-, Tom Arnold, Ivor Benbow, Dai Davies ('Dai, She Faints'), John Rowsell. Kneeling: Arthur Benbow, Emrys James. Dai Davies kept a shop and one day a young boy working for him ran in to the shop and announced that Dai's wife had fainted, 'Dai, she faints'. People in the shop heard this and the phrase stuck with him as a nickname for the rest of his life. The shop is still in Bute Street and to this day is known as 'Dai, She Faints' shop!

Laying the foundation stones of Treherbert Cottage Hospital, 19 April 1927.

Bethany Baptist chapel ladies choir, 1953. From left to right, back row: Myra Williams, Enid Morgan, Marion Barclay, Dilys James, Ann Benbow, Burl Morgan, Doreen James, Ann Bowen, Nesta James, Iris Davies. Front row: Dorothy Hughes, Mivie Morse, Gwenno Coles, Audrey James, Maureen Thomas, Rosemary Coles, Marion Purdle, Pamela Williams, Hilary Lancey.

The Black and White Toppers jazz band led by Emma Bryant (bandleader), marching through Dunraven Street. Note the Stuart Hotel on the left, c. 1954.

Members of Treherbert Maes-yr-Haf day outing at Southsea, *c.* 1959. On the far side of the front table, from the right: Nellie Jenkins, Maria Timothy, -?-, Mrs Bowen, Annie May Jones, Mavis Green, Mrs Davies. On the near side of the table, from front to back, Mrs Jones from Swansea (obscured), Jinny Evans, -?-, -?-, Mrs Howells.

Sol Watkins' New Road garage, 1949. From left to right, back row: John Jones, Glyn Jones, George Alder. Front row: Kidd Watkins, Gwyn Jenkins, Alan Jones, -?-.

Members celebrate the centenary of the Libanus chapel, 1940.

A Rhondda Chamber of Trade dance at Driscoll's club in Porth 30 January 1964. From left to right: Ron James, Megan James, Eirwen Hawkins, Will Scott, Kitty Scott, Tom Page, Mary Greenhill, Cyril Greenhill, Mavis Page, Jack Hawkins.

Staff of Treherbert Secondary Modern boys' school. From left to right, back row: Ernest Oliver, John Morris, -?-, Ossie Morgan, Dilwyn Thomas, Charlie Evans. Front row: Tom Duggan, Mr 'Potty' Pearce, Mr Lewis (headmaster), Pyer Davies, Jack Haddock.

School cricket team 1948. From left to right, back row: -?-, Ken Parry, -?-, Ken Farmer, Tommy Morgan. Middle row: ? Warren, Gordon Jones, John Townsend, Dai Aubrey, Mick Powell. Front row: Mr Lewis (headmaster), Morlais Adams, Edwin Parry, John Sampson, Ken Watts, Ernest Oliver (teacher).

Members of the school swimming class, 1948/9. From left to right, back row: -?-, Colin Morgan, Glan Davies, -?-, Emlyn Davies, Phil Rees, Bryn Price, David Quelch. Second row: Danny Pyer, John Rees, -?-, Charles Ellis, Howard Davies, Billy Spurway, Billy Evans, -?-. Third row: Mr Thomas (teacher), Arwyn Davies, John Jasper, Terry Berry, Mr Lewis (headmaster), David Evans, Eddy White, John Howells, Mr Morris (teacher). Front row: Ken John, Jimmy Shanklyn, Danny Morgan, -?-, Andy Parry, John Jones.

School rugby team, 1948. From left to right, back row: Alan Pickens, -?-, George Rees, Tom Thomas, Gwyn Richards, Malcom Owen, Ray Evans, Brian Peasely, John Townsend. Middle row: Charlie Evans (teacher), John Lee, John Sampson, Morlais Edwards, Mr Lewis (headmaster), Ivor Jones, Caradoc Lewis, Gordon Jones, Pyer Davies (teacher). Front row: Tommy Morgan, Dai Aubrey, Ken Parry, Donald Fisher, Edwin Parry, Viv Price.

A mock-up carnival tramcar advertising businesses in Treherbert, *c.* 1925. Note the step ladder used for the stairs!

Five

Penyrenglyn and Ynyswen

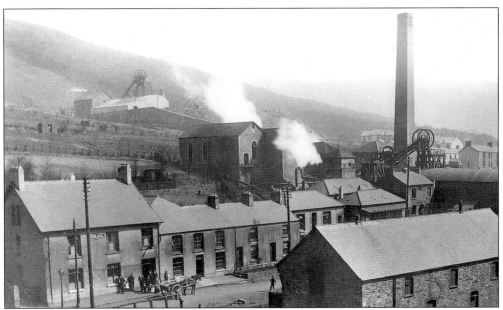

Ynysofeio Colliery, Treherbert, 1910. Note the horse and cart outside the Baglan Hotel and the stables in the right hand corner.

Rhys Evans and his family of Baglan Street, *c.* 1904. From left to right, standing: John Price Evans (son-in-law), Tommy (son), Ben Jones (son-in-law), Seated: Elizabeth Evans (daughter), William (grandson), Rhys Evans, Baban (baby granddaughter), Ossie Jones (grandson), Annie Jane Jones (daughter).

The Dutfield family, Percy and Louise with children Rene, Eric and Bill. They were the owners of a grocery shop at 7 Ynyswen Road in 1915.

The Crown public house, 1912. Notice the Palace cinema bill in the window advertising the laying in state of General Booth, founder of the Salvation Army.

Carmel chapel soup kitchen, 1921.

Standard 2 of Penyrenglyn girls' school, 1913.

Standard 3a of Ynyswen infants school, 1913.

Standard 1 of Ynyswen council school, 1913. From left to right, front row: Alfie Miles, Harold White, Cyril Williams, Ted Richards, ? Hinton, Morgan Jeremiah, Eddie James, Haydn Davies, Ivor Williams, Eddie Jones, Cyril Carpenter, Thomas John Williams, Harold Russ. Second row: W.H. Owen (headmaster), Wynford Jones, Peter Angel, Eben Salathiel, -?-, Eddie Owen, Owen Davies, ? Evans, ? Brew, -?-, -?-, Lionel Jacka, Tommy Richards, George Cambourne, Harold Wilson, Frank Isles (teacher). Third row: Joe Morgan (Sol), Isaac Martin, Emlyn Hughes, -?-, Percy Beynon, Percy Fews, ? Foulkes, -?-, Caradoc Gwilym, George John, -?-, Noah Thomas, David Elwyn Jones, Gordon Harvey Jones, -?-. Back row: Charles Jenkins, Joseph Jones, Will Harries, ? Griffiths, Percy Hogan, Emlyn Millward, Edwin Perry, Walt Martin, John Miles, -?-, -?-, Christie Davies, -?-, Bob John, Cyril Evans.

Ynyswen school concert for Netely hospital, April 1916.

Left: Ellen Mary (Nellie) Hughes age ten years, dressed for St Davids day, 1923. *Right:* Private Hugh Hughes, !st Monmouthshire Regiment, 1 September 1917. Ellen and Hugh lived at 1 Ynysofeio Avenue.

Penyrenglyn infants class, 3b, 1931. Included in the photograph are, back row: Tommy Howells, Donald Phillips, Stanley Husband. Middle row: Thelma Dutfield, Pamela Kinsey, Stella Hughes, Audrey Hughes, Rita Morgan, Iris Luscombe. Front row: Elsie Axford, Jennie Owen (holding board), Iris Barnes, Beryl Price.

Treherbert Town football team. From left to right, standing: -?-, Glyn Jones, Rupert Jones, A. Booton, Jim Wilkins, Harry Gratehead, Tom Jones, Phip Jones, Will Thomas (Ty-Fleming), Joe Bevan. Second row: -?-, Jack Jones, -?-, Walter Moon, Ianto Davies (Aberystwyth), Idris Tasker. Front row: Ivor Davies (Cwm), Ike ?, -?-, -?-, Will Moon.

Ynyswen AFC, 1926/27.

All Saints church choir, c. 1938. From left to right, back row: -?-, -?-, John Hughes (choirmaster), Rice Lewis (vicar), ? Collins. Second row: ? Collins, Tilly Wynne, Brenda Lewis, Joyce Davies, ? Beech, ? Warren, -?-, Donald Phillips, -?-. Third row: -?-, -?-, Olwen Roberts, Beryl Gregory, Doreen Jones, Joyce Phillips, Stella Hinks, Olwen Hughes, Iris Luscombe, Betty Thomas, -?-. Front row, Betty Wynne, Sylvia Williams, Valmai Jones, Maisie Luscombe, Marjorie Sheppard, Joan West, Audrey Evans, Mary Lewis, Sadie Cull, May Phillips.

A large number of Penyrenglyn residents on a sports day on the Baglan field, 1943. They are standing on the old tip.

A fair on the Baglan field, (after the tip had been removed), celebrating the change of status from the Rhondda Urban District Council to Rhondda Borough Council.

The First Aid team at a ladies footbal match celebrating Prince Charles' investiture as Prince of Wales, July 1969. Left to right: Terry Lewis (in the chair), Betty Partridge, Doreen Jenkins.

Day trip of members of the Upper Rhondda Workingmens Club to the CIU rest home at Langland Bay. From left to right, back row: Les Rees, Mavine Richy, ? Lourie, Nipper Collins, -?-, Griff Evans, Idris Jones, -?-, -?-, Tommy Jones. Second row: Louvain Manic, -?-, Ken Bassett, -?-, Rhys Hunt, Mo Lewis, Bob Morris, Vince Edwards, Dai Drake, Geraint Phillips. Third row: Bert Jones, Lal Jones, Dennis O' Conner, Mr O' Conner, Cyril Thomas, Mrs Thomas, -?-, Mary Edwards, -?-, -?-, Jack Mannie, Jenny Phillips. Front row: Olive Hunt, Enid Evans, Van Bassett, Lawrence Richy, -?-, Esme Rees, -?-, Mrs Lewis.

Polikoff Gleemen, February 1951. From left to right, back row: -?-, D. Morgan, L. Jones. -?-, K. Moon, S. James, B. Jones, -?-, -?-, F. Williams, -?-, -?-, J. Meredith, G. Beynon. Middle row: M. Thomas, E. Thomas, T. Bailey, -?-, J. Pitt, G. Excel, E. Chapman, A. Parker, M. Rees, J. Sully, -?-, J. Griffiths, -?-, H. Williams. Front row: D. Livingstone, D. Jeremiah, G. Jones, R. Excel, D. Jones (conductor), P. Hanley, -?-, K. Richards,-?-, D. Jones.

Six
Treorchy

The Cardiff Arms hotel and square, *c.* 1904. The hotel was used as the headquarters of the Treorchy rugby club. Cemetry Road can be seen in the background.

A view of the lower end of Treorchy showing Cae mawr and Ystradfechan fields before developement, *c.* 1920. The railway station and goods yard can clearly be seen in the foreground and Pentre in the background.

A boxing exhibition, on the site of Pencelli bowling green, between Jimmy Wilde and Shaun Price, *c.* 1913.

The Samuel family who lived at 152 Dumfries Street, *c.* 1912. From left to right, back row: Thomas, Elizabeth, Samuel, Margaret, Rachel, William Henry. Middle row: Jonathan, Anna May, William, Anna, David, Ellen. Front row: Edith, Violet, Gertrude, Trevor, Stanley, Blodwen.

The first wedding at Gosen chapel 1919. From left to right, back row: Thomas Jones, Edith Jones, William Samuels, Gertrude Samuels, Emrys Jones. Front row: Elizabeth Jones, Thomas Samuel, Blodwen Samuel, David John Owen, -?-. In front: Violet Samuel.

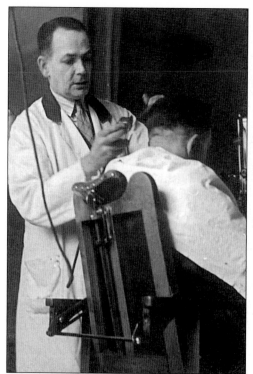

Above left: Tom Jones (barber), cutting the hair of Mr Porter, who kept a sweetshop in Station Sreet, *c.* 1949. *Above right:* Children of Rees street, 1944. Left to right: Maldwyn Bees, Arthur Kinsey, Ceri Kinsey. In front: Peter Hunt, Nellie Edmunds, Ann Pomeroy.

Ned Jones who won the Welsh wrestling championship 8 November 1919, with Ivor (Nippy) Williams from Ynyswen. Ivor emigrated to America and was known as Doc Williams through his ability as a masseur. He was also photographed with Tommy Farr at Long Beach, New Jersey in 1937.

Standard 5a at Treorchy Junior school, 1931. From left to right, back row: Ellis Thomas, George Newman, Keri Davies, Will Hadley, Jack Morris, Eddy Ashton, Cled Lewis, Norman Jones, Picton Rees, Des Davies, Norman Haddock. Second row: W.B. Cleaver (pupil teacher), Haydn Jones, Bert Millward, Eddy Goodhall, Tudor Owen, Treharne Jones, Dan Evans, Cliff Holley, Ted Nicholas, John Dyer, Idris Davies, Raymond Hughes (teacher). Third row: George Smith, Cyril Jones, Ken Williams, Will Woodward, Ernie Joynes, Jim Hier, Syd Mathias, Cyril Shepherd, Ken Hollow, Ken Bassett, Idris Morris. Front row: John Thomas, Vic Clarke, Vaynor Thomas, Tal Williams, Haydn Davies, Ivor Morgan, Des Jones, Glan Reynolds, Idris White, Haydn Evans, Trevor Davies, Miss Davis (headmistress).

Celebrating VE Day, 1945. Left to right: David Jones, Colin Williams, Alan Quirke, outside Tom Jones' barbers shop at 172 Bute Street.

High Street, *c*. 1900. Next to the Bethlehem chapel at No. 26 is David Evan Davies the chemist. The barbers pole on the right is No. 187, David George the hairdresser.

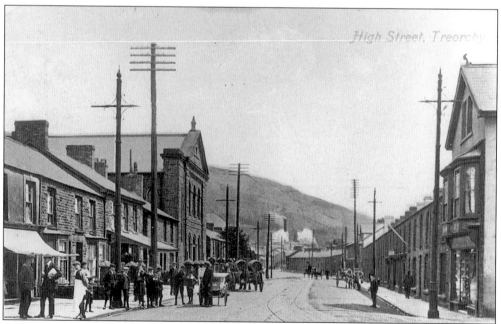

High Street, *c*. 1910. The cart outside the chapel is a vinegar cart. Notice the steam rising from Tynybedw colliery in the background.

Bottom end of High Street, *c.* 1912. The shop on the right hand side, No. 159/160, is Morgan Bros, drapers. Note the tramcar opposite the Red Cow hotel.

The top end of High Street, *c.* 1912. The chemist shop at No 26 is now George Radford's billiard room. The chemist shop moved over the road to No. 204.

Pentwyn hospital medical staff, 1925. Standing in the cenre is Dr Armstrong and seated is Will John MP for Rhondda West.

Pentwyn hospital staff, 1925.

Pentwyn hospital Board of Management, 1925.

Pentwyn Cottage Hospital medical and nursing staff, April 1948. From left to right, standing: Winifred Evans (cook), A.J. Fox, Nancy Meredith, Phyllis John, Joan Cousins, Ethel Roberts, Betty Thomas, Mair Lewis, Mrs M. Jones, Glyn Thomas (gardener), Eleanor Davies. Seated: Sister Miriam Harris, Dr J. Jones, Dr W.A. Burke, Matron Olwen Lewis, Dr Fergus Armstrong, Dr A.M. Robertson, Nesta Jones.

Glamorgan Special Constabulary, 'G' Division, Treorchy section, 22 October 1944. From left to right, back row: J. Thomas, G. Morris, -?-, -?-, ? Jones, ? Reynolds, C. Higgon, A. Davies. Second row: Mr Vaughan, D. Jones, O. Jones, ? Picton, A. Spiller, T. Eynon, -?-, ? Hopkins, -?-, Fred Vaughan, -?-. Third row: -?-, E. Thomas, E. Davies, -?-, W. Powell, -?-, I. Phillips, ? Reid, -?-, F. George, G. Oram, T.D. Griffiths. Front row: D. Edwards, H. Wood, D. Wood, Sgt Moore, Insp. T. Jones, Insp. Evans, Insp. F. Evans, M. Hughes, D. Davies, T. Jones, T. Davies.

Glamorgan Special Constabulary, Senior Officers of 'G' Division, July 1945. From left to right, standing: N. Griffiths, W. Prosser, O. Cule, A. John, A. Demaid, W. Rees, W. Edwards, G. Jones. Seated: E. Latham, G. Howell, E. Thomas, W.M. Davies, C. O'Brien, F. Evans, T. Jones, D. Davies. Inset; W. Bateman.

CHILDRENS' PLAYGROUND, TREORCHY.

Childrens playground, *c.* 1940.

RAFA Club Tramps Ball. Owen Thomas stands at the back (with pint in hand), then, from left to right, back: Colin Trowell (wearing bowler), Gwyn Davies, Margaret Davies, Tom Hughes, Gordon Richards. At front, left: Dai Morgan (wearing trilby hat), Ellen Hughes, Eifion Williams, -?-, Mrs Davies, Betty Jones, Des Jones, Joan Richards. In front, Em Jenkins (with beard), Marion Mason, Margaret Morgan, Maureen Williams.

Boys club soccer team, 1930/31. From left to right, backrow: -?-, Phil Haines, Reg Stuckey, Cecil Edwards, -?-, -?-, -?-. Second row: Bill Richards, -?-, Ivor Samuel, Arthur Williams, Arthur Harry. Front row: Bill Pritchard, Arthur Powell, Islwyn Bowen.

Royal Welsh Male Choir (Treorchy), 1927. From left to right, back row; Gomer Williams (tenor soloist), Steve James (tenor soloist), Wm J. Dickson (baritone soloist), Tom Thomas (elocutionist). Sitting; Gwilym T. Jones, (musical director), Richard Davies (accompanist), D. Davies, (base soloist).

Peglers' stores, 203 High street, *c.* 1955. From left to right, David John Rees (manager), Tommy ?, Jack Jones, Sylvia Griffiths, Bryn Edwards, Beryl Davies.

Glyncoli House, Treorchy CS school, 1952/53. From left to right, back row: Sheila Noakes,-?-, Maureen Trott, Eirwen Turner, Betty Noakes, Ruth Jones, David Pugh, -?-, Brian Williams, Vernon Thomas, Keith Holmes. Second row: -?-, -?-, -?-, Eileen Smith, Barbara Howells, Vivienne Hammond, Ken Thomas, Russel Eveson, David Seal, -?-, David Oliver, John Skym, Alwyn Edwards. Third row: -?-, Margaret Waite, -?-, Ann Eveson, Marion Jones, Pat Powell, -?-, Alethia Glass, Byron Morgan, John Chapman, David Reynolds, Glen Holmes, Meirion John, Ken Evans, John Bowen. Fourth row: Marion Rees, -?-, Anne Jones, Pat Davidson, Muriel Lewis, Diane Evans, Dilys Jones, David Jones, Elsie Samuel, Cyril Evans, Sheila Walters, Paul Blake, Meirion Owen, Robert Bonner, Brian Smith, Clifford Fennel, Graham Blaydon, -?-, Idris Jones (Cedric). Front row: Gillian Bell, -?-, Anne Williams, Betty Merriman, Bernice Powell, Beryl Downes, -?-, Marlene Edwards, Margaret Evans, Morgan Edwards, Tony Gillard, Alwyn Blaydon, Roy Trott, David James, Tom Eveson, Peter Jones.

Pentwyn Cottage Hospital, opened in January 1925, is now a private nursing home. Note Pentre Seconday school in the background.

Noddfa Baptist chapel, c. 1904. Above the second shop on the right hand side was the Barmouth Temperance rooms.

Treorchy 'All Whites' rugby team, *c.* 1925. Seated in the middle row, sixth from left, is Dick Newman.

Treorchy Boys Club team, 1932. From left to right, back row: Ned Knapgate, Trevor Rees, Tim Fitzpatrick, Will Williams, -?-, ? Wilcox, ? Jones, Evan Erasmus. Middle row: ? Hughes, Phil Haines, Fred Morgan, Danny Hughes, Phil Evans, Harry Mars. Front row: -?-, Harry Jones (Hermon), Tom Granfield, Cliff Knapgate.

EMI factory, *c.* 1960. Included in the photograph are, Glan Williams, Trevor Lewis, Bryn John, George Carp, Tom Jones, Phil Hamer, Ray Soley, Stan Jones, David Davies, Freddy Bevan, Dai Roberts, Wally Codling.

Abergorky Colliery No.3 Rescue Brigade, 1913. Standing: H. Thorne, Jos Owen, W.M. Goodall, Lewis Scourfield, Supt.Thorne. Kneeling: Rees Davies, Evan Thomas (captain), James Owen.

Seven

Cwmparc

Andy Capp and Flo painted on the council building at the top of Bwlch mountain road at the junction with Blaengwynfi and Nantymoel. Although this building has been demolished the cycle race authorities still refer to it as 'Andy Capp' on their race route.

Standard 4 at Cwmparc boys school, 1931. From left to right, back row: Evan Rees, Owen Rutledge, Ron Thomas, George Davies (pointing to his lapel badge awarded for having clean hands), Teddy Davidson, -?-, Albert Nut, Haydn Morgan, George Davies (RAFA), -?-, Mel Davies. Second row: Mr Cleaver, -?-, -?-, Tom Mackie, -?-, Gwilym James, Bill Thomas, -?-, Spencer Bevan, Jack Watkins, Dilwyn Evans, Bill Davies, Mr Thomas. Third row: Cyril Veal, Reg Lewis, -?-, Tom Jones, Mel Williams, Oliver Godfrey, -?-, -?-, -?-, -?-, -?-. Front row: -?-, -?-, Ron Williams, -?-, Will Williams (holding board), Frankie Cox, -?-, -?-, Merlyn Jones.

Parc infants school, 'babies' class, 1931.

Form 2 at Cwmparc boys' school, 1931.

Standard 5a at Cwmparc boys' school, 1931. From left to right, back row: Jackie Baker, Robert Lloyd, Ron Evans, Llew Evans, Ken Lewis, Archie North, Syd Ferguson, Jim Morris, Stan James. Second row: Gomer Evans (headmaster), Ken Hughes, Dickie Owen, Rob Watkins, Roy Morgan, Cliff Bound, Ray Davies, -?-, Gwyn Hughes, Dick Lewis, -?-. Third row: Ellis Williams, Dai Jones, Jack Jones, Ken Higgs, Jack Whitelead, Handel MIllward, Ken Hughes, Jack Morris, Ernie Taylor. Front row: Gwyn Davies, Teged Jones, Robert Duggan, Dai George, Bill Field, -?-, Syd Ashton, Bill Harding.

Parc Colliery, 7 January 1967. Note the line of rubbish tips going up the side of the mountain. The colliery closed later that year.

General view of Cwmparc, c. 1919.

1st Cwmparc BP Wolf Cubs, 1922. Included in the photograph are: Will J. Evans, Dick O'Brien, Jack O' Brien, Jack Leakey, Amos Rodgers, Sydney Lewis, David Hafod Jones, Willie Ross, Glyn Thomas, Trevor Thomas, Billy Hughes, Cubmaster George White (centre, with hat), Jack O'Brien (assistant).

St Georges church choir, *c.* 1930. The vicar is G. Shilton Evans. Included in the photograph are: Edgar Evans, Stan Powell, Gwyn Aubrey, Eira Owen, Bob Meredith, Harold Hooper, Tom Davies, Jack Williams, Ivor Jones, Dan Spencer, Ivor Williams (organist), Walter Williams, Mr Nottage, Terry Jones, Donald Carpenter, Jamie Dundridge, Winnie Farmer, Marion Jones, Nettie Howells, Mrs Hawkins, Gwenny Evans, Mrs Spencer, Brynhilda Evans, Kate Meredith.

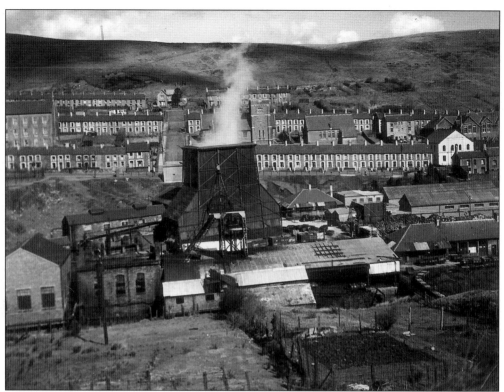

Dare Colliery, *c.* 1960.

The landscaped site of Dare Colliery, after its closure in 1964 and before the building of the Alicia day centre. The centre was named after Alice Boxhall, former borough councillor and mayor.

Members of the Bethel chapel perfomance of *Zuruika the Gypsy Maid*, 1945. Included in the cast are, Eunice Powell, Hetty Weaver, Emrys Lloyd, Roy Williams, Margaret Hamer, Gwyn Gregory, Haydn Curtiss, Marina Kinsey, Mair Jones, Maudie Haye, Jack Jones, Muriel Rees, Margaret Thomas, Pat Chambers, Rosemary Evans, Emlyn Jones, Barbara Williams, Mair Thomas, Ann Jones, Megan Campbell, Joy Painter, Betty Griffiths, Muriel Lewis, Priscilla Evans, Rachel Grant, Diane Evans, Janet Jones.

Leading members of the cast of *Zuruika the Gypsy Maid*. From left to right, Mair Thomas, Maudie Haye, Jack Jones, -?-, Rosemary Evans, Muriel Rees, Maureen ?. Seated: Haydn Curtiss, -?-.

Pencelli Stars AFC, 1920/21.

Parc colliery wagonshop football team, played in Pentwyn Hospital Cup, 1941/2. From left to right, back row: Will Price (referee), Ninian Join, Ivor Owen, Frank Steadman, Albert Stubbs, Orlando Jones, -?-, Jackie Morgan. Middle row: Russ Reynolds, Jack Knapgate, Ike Pearce, Don Morris, George Reynolds, Cliff Knapgate, Dick Griffiths. Front row: Dai Thomas, -?-, -?-, Charlie Hawkins.

Parc colliery No.1 pit football team, winners of Pentwyn Hospital Cup, 1941/2. From left to right, back row: Tom Alf Davies, ? Fitzgerald, Edgar Jones. Middle row: Cyril Shepherd, Jack Mars, Stan Boxhall, Alec Boxhall. Front row: Jack Roberts, Garfield Cadwgan, Tommy Evans (Saunders), Gwyn Reynolds, Will Richards (Rich), Harold Pritchard. The man on the far right (in slouch hat) is thought to be the General Manager of Ocean Coal Company. Seated: Maggie Rees, -?-.

Cwmparc AFC, 1952. From left to right, standing: Eddie Morgan, Fred (Curly) Thomas, Peter Elson, Ken Wilson, Roy Whitbread, Mansel Kettley, Roy Jones, Mansel Samuels. Seated: Wally Nash, Les Lowry, -?-, -?-, Em Thomas, Trevor Davies.

Children of Railway Terrace, *c.* 1925. From left to right, back row, Tegwen Jones, Mary Turner, Mrs Tomkinson, -?-, -?-, -?-, -?-, Mrs Davies, -?-. Middle row: -?-, Ronnie Jones, Jimmy Grant, Ritchie Holmes, Tommy Grant, -?-, -?-, Evan Morgan. Seated: -?-, Dai Griffiths, Roy Jeremiah, Maggie May Grant, Mary Ann Grant, -?-, -?-, -?-.

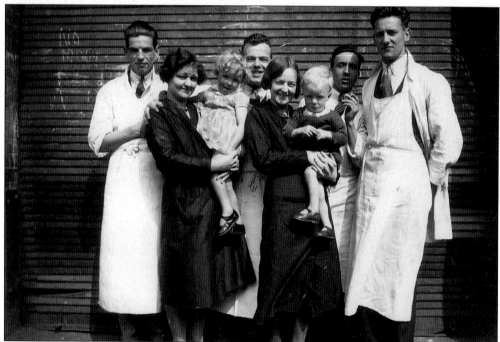

Cwmparc branch of Ton Cooperative, *c.* 1932. From left to right, Percy Mantle, Gwyneth Davies (holding Mair Morgan), -?-, -?-, Howell Morgan (held), -?-, -?-.

Standard 4a of Parc girls' school, 1931. The teacher is Olwen Edwards who was also the conductress of Polikoffs' girls choir.

Employees of the NCB wagon repair shop shortlly before its closure in 1959. From left to right, back row: Frank Lloyd, Emyr Jones, Jack Bowen, Dick Griffiths, Emlyn Thomas, George Stephens, Will Lloyd, David Jones, Idris Cousins, Gwilym Morgan, Glyn Daniels, Derek Walters. Middle row: Arthur Richardson, Islwyn Price, David Jenkins, Sam Latcham, David Thomas, Glyn Wigley, Joe Latcham, David Bowen, Syd Ball, Alwyn Phillips, Eddie Rowe, John H.Williams, Rhys Morgan Rees. Front row: Cyril Davies, Meirion John, Roy Richards, David Davies, Aneurin Reynolds, Keith Griffiths, Jackie Rees, Orlando Jones, Eilyr Wright. Kneeling/sitting: Michael Jones, Glyn Jones.

Cwmparc St Johns Ambulance Division, 1963/64. From left to right: Eddy Morgan, George Morgan, Eli Jones, Commisioner McTiffin, Evan Jones, Gwilym Phillips.

Cwmparc unemployed club, 21 June 1950. From left to right, back row: Phyllis Wilcox, Li Humphrey, Mrs Bebb, Blod Brown, Beatty Holmes, Margaret Curtiss. Middle row: Mrs Hall, Mrs.Thomas, -?-, Elizabeth Ann Clayton. Front row: Edie May Rees, Megan Vaughan, Enneline Fitzpatrick, -?-, Gwyneth John.

A group of players from the Parc & Dare band collecting for the distress fund for locked out miners in South Wales during the 1921 General Strike. From left to right, back row: Evan H. Evans, Haydn Bebb, Ted Evans, Lewis Brown. Seated: Evan Owen, W.Holland, Rufus Jones (bandmaster), John Evans, Joe Owen. Front row: Percy Price, Emrys Watkins.

The complete Parc & Dare band at the *Daily Herald* contest in the Albert Hall, 1945. The band won third place.

Left: Myra Thomas and John Tyler performing *Elijah* at Parc hall, 1954. *Right:* Members of Parc & Dare band at Cardiff, 1937. From left to right, Ted Edwards (cornet), Haydn Bebb (conductor), Lewis Brown (flugel horn).

Cwmparc AFC, 1960. From left to right, standing: Eddie Morgan, Roy Whitbread, Gwyn Evans, Les Lowry, Ron Jones, Bill Paul, Ken Wilson. Kneeling: Em Thomas, Hedley Curtiss (captain), Alby Curtiss, Cyril Mills, Owen Davies.

Standard 5 of Parc girls' school, 1936. Included in the photograph are: Pat Townsend, Pheoni Tortello, Miss Sadie Davies (teacher), Betty Clayton.

Form 2 of Parc boys' school, 1936. From left to right, back row: Tom Jones, Tommy Mackey, Johnny Breeze, -?-, Ossie Holmes, Billy Field, ? Price. Second row: Ernie Oliver (teacher), Arthur Searle, -?-, Stan James, -?-, ? Bevan, Alfie Cox, Eddie Davies, D.R. Rees (headmaster). Third row: ? Rowlands, Stanley Adams, -?-, David Price, -?-, David Watkins, Stanley Bevan. Front row: Handel Bevan, -?-, Tommy Thomas, Eddie Roberts, Alfie Thomas.

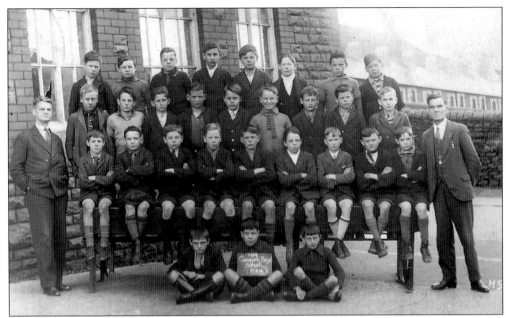

Standard 2 of Cwmparc boys' school, 1929. Included in the photograph are: Herbert Evans, Harry Gillard, Will Thomas, Jeffrey Jones, Sydney Price, Morgan Lewis, Doug Pugh, Billy Williams, Ron Whittaker. On the left is Gomer Evans (headmaster), on the right is Rufus Ashton (teacher).

Group 2b, 1st class of Cwmparc school, 1902.

Gwyneth John (née Clayton), at five years old, *c.* 1912.

Acknowledgements

The authors would like to thank a large number of individuals and organizations for their help in the compilation of this book. Without their assistance it would not have been possible to present this photographic history of the area in all its rich variety. We sincerely apologize to anyone who has helped us over the years and has been inadvertently omitted from the following list:

Maralyn Balestrazzi, D.J. Barber, John Brown, Ellen Butcher, Annie Clarke, George Davies, Arwyn Davies, Megan Davies, John Davies, Howard Davies, W.J. Evans (Butch), Enid Evans, Gladys Gardner, Helen Horgan, Herbert Hunt, Ellen Hughes, Meirion John, Irene Johnson, David Jones, Cyril John, Olive Jones, Annie May Jones, Burl Jones, Betty Jackson, Catherine Jones, Ron Jones, Eddie Morgan, Jean Morgan, Vera Morgan, Mavis Page, Ena Parry, Margaret Phillips, Gwyn Phillips, Bill Phillips, Sian Poppham, Albert Stubbs, Will Scott, Arthur Spiller, John Smith, Jean Vaughan, Stephen Winter, Stella Walters, Barbara Ware, Fred Williams, Blaencwm, Blaenrhondda, and Dunraven schools, Haydn Bundock, Danny Walters, Trevor Hitchings, Catering Manager, (upgraded from tea boy). Our special thanks go to the committee of the OAP Hall for the use of their hall, and last but not least, to our wives Doreen Jenkins and Mavis Green for their patience and understanding.

Thank you for looking back at our valley. I cross my legs hoping that you will return again!